THIRTEEN REASONS WHY
YOU BELONG

THIRTEEN REASONS

WHY YOU

BELONG

An Honoring of Adolescence

TARA EMRICK

HIP
ME
Publishing

Denver, Co

Thirteen Reasons Why You Belong:
An Honoring of Adolescence

Published by HIP ME Publishing
Denver, CO

Book cover design by Victoria Wolf. Interior design by Michelle M. White.
Author Photograph by Jennifer Minor.

Paperback ISBN: 978-1-7337395-0-4
Hardcover ISBN: 978-1-7337395-1-1

YOUNG ADULT NONFICTION /
Social Topics / Self-Esteem & Self-Reliance

QUANTITY PURCHASES: Schools, companies, professional groups, clubs, and other organizations may qualify for special terms when ordering quantities of this title. For information, email info@hipMePublishing.com.

Many of the tools and techniques explained in this book were taught to the author by others and were not created by the author. All of the tools and techniques are offered as suggestions. They are not meant to replace professional mental health support. *Thirteen Reasons Why You Belong* is not meant to be used in place of therapy. Please seek professional help if you feel like hurting yourself or someone else.

Dedication

For Matt (1979–2006)
Your light and love continue to transform so many lives.
I will miss you forever.

CONTENTS

INTRODUCTION

WHAT DOES IT MEAN TO BELONG?

When I asked my teenage daughter what it means to belong, she said, "Belonging means I am supposed to be here."

I AM SUPPOSED TO BE HERE.

Then I asked her if she feels like she belongs, and she said, "Sometimes." I imagine most of us feel the same way. Sometimes we feel like we are supposed to be here, and sometimes we do not. There are certain times in our lives when we can especially struggle to feel like we belong. Our teenage years tend to be such a time.

So, now here you are in your teen years. You are no longer a child. You are a teenager, and you are now part of a new community, a new group.

This transition, or passage, into being a teenager can be exciting, scary, confusing, painful, messy, and joyous. It is *so normal* to wonder who you are, why you are here, if you are supposed to be here, and why you matter. It is *so normal* to wonder if you belong and to feel like you don't. The truth is you have ALWAYS belonged. You have always belonged because you are here on purpose, you are meant to be here, and that reason for being is what makes you belong.

My hope for you, as you enter this new life chapter, is to know this: you have a purpose, and you are here for a reason. My hope for you is that you begin to remember you belong here because you are divine, which basically means you are connected to all beings in a beautiful and powerful way.

> "Tell me, what is it you plan to do with your one wild and precious life?"
> ~ Mary Oliver

The reason I say "begin to remember" is because many of us forget soon after we are born that we are connected to each other and to something greater than ourselves. There are several reasons for this forgetting, which we will talk about later. The main focus here is to let yourself start to remember that we do in fact belong, that we are all connected, and that our one precious life, as Mary Oliver writes about, is invaluable!

It is okay to question this connection, to doubt this, to not believe it or not understand it. Maybe the "thirteen reasons" are simply an invitation to open yourself up to the possibility that YOU matter, that your life matters, that you are here for a reason. If that is the case, I hope you honor this invitation by opening up your heart to the possibilities and suggestions presented in the following pages. To the words and ideas expressed. To using one or more of the tools presented. To committing to a daily practice. Using one or more of the tools offered can become a daily practice, which means you apply that tool to your every-day life until it becomes a habit.

I invite you to read through the *Thirteen Reasons Why You Belong* and see which reason or reasons speak the loudest to you. Maybe you read one reason a day and sit with it. Maybe you use the tool suggested in that chapter and see how you feel about it before you move on to the next reason. There is no right or wrong way to read this book. Take a risk, open your heart, and see where it takes you.

YOU BELONG BECAUSE
YOUR MIND IS POWERFUL
AND YOUR THOUGHTS ARE POWERFUL

WHY ARE OUR THOUGHTS SO POWERFUL?

Most of us live in our heads. Most of us have a running inner dialogue, also known as that voice in our head that talks to us constantly. This is normal. Our mind and our thoughts help us to live every day. Our mind helps us decide when it's safe to cross the street. Our mind helps us communicate with other people, helps us use our phones and computers, helps us learn in school, and helps us function on a daily basis. Our mind and our thoughts are important, and they are very powerful.

That power can be both good and bad. If we have positive thoughts running through our head, they can help us navigate daily life with love, strength, courage, and belief in ourselves. If we have negative thoughts running through our head, they can get in the way of us finding joy, living as our real selves, or noticing how we truly feel in the present moment. They can definitely get in the way of connecting to ourselves and each other.

It is normal to go from positive to negative thoughts throughout the day. The problem is that most of us get caught up in our negative thoughts much more often than the positive ones. Frequently, our running internal dialogue is filled with comparisons of ourselves to others, judgment of ourselves, judgment of others, and beliefs that everything and everyone is separate from us, all of which causes us to doubt ourselves. That doubt can lead us to question what we are capable of. That doubt can lead us to feel really bad about ourselves.

> "I suffer from low self-esteem. I had horrible self-esteem growing up. You really have to save yourself because the critic within you will eat you up. It's not the outside world—it's your interior life, that critic within you, that you have to silence."
> ~ Iman

It is easy to focus on how we do not measure up to everyone else. It is easy to focus on our weaknesses. It is also easy to focus on being stressed out and overwhelmed. These stressed-out thoughts take us from being in our bodies and keep us stuck in our heads. This is a problem because we are not *just* our heads. We are our bodies too, and within our bodies lie our hearts. The more we live in our bodies and our hearts, the more we become aware of our connection to ourselves, each other, and the natural world. The way to strengthen that awareness is through noticing or paying attention to our thoughts.

How do we notice our thoughts and take back that running dialogue in our head?

This takes LOTS of practice because we live in a society where we are encouraged to live in our heads, to be controlled by that running dialogue, and to be judgmental and critical of ourselves and others. It's okay to practice judgment and to have opinions. Critical thinking is not the problem. The problem is when that judgment ends up separating us from ourselves and from others. The problem is when we put people, including ourselves, into one of two categories: good or bad.

For example, there is nothing wrong with the critical thoughts, "Those are cute jeans" or "Those are ugly jeans." We all have opinions. The problem arises when we continue beyond that thought and work our way into a story we tell ourselves—that either makes us feel bad about ourselves or makes us feel that another person is bad.

Our initial thought, "Those are cute jeans," then goes into a running dialogue of, "Too bad I can't buy those jeans. It's not fair that I can't buy those jeans. It wouldn't really matter if I could buy those jeans because they wouldn't look good on me anyway. My thighs are too big to look good in those jeans ... blah blah blah ..." See how easily our thoughts get away from us?

Or the other critical thought, "Those are ugly jeans," can go from that single thought to, "Those jeans look terrible on her. Why is she wearing those jeans? What made her think she could pull off that look? I'm going to roll my eyes at her and make sure she knows that she should not be wearing those jeans ... blah, blah, blah ..." A single critical thought can spiral into a tornado of negative thoughts and feelings.

None of the thoughts and feelings in either scenario is founded in love. They do not help us feel better about ourselves or others. They may help us make sense of something in the moment, but over time, the negativity rooted in those thoughts brings us down. And the energy associated with such negative thoughts stays with us long after the physical moment or experience is over.

It's up to us to turn our negative thoughts into positive ones. This is *not* the same thing as thinking that everything is good and wonderful all of the time. Terrible, sad, and horrible things do happen. We have thoughts and feelings around those experiences too. The idea here is that we find a way to identify and genuinely express what we are thinking and feeling, both positive and negative, and then work to practice more positive, loving, and healing thoughts about ourselves and others throughout the day.

A good place to start is through loving self-talk. Look for moments throughout your day to practice loving self-talk by creating an "I am statement," which is sometimes referred to as a *mantra* (a Sanskrit word for a little phrase you say to yourself repeatedly that you want to start believing about yourself or manifesting in your life). Your *mantra* could be something like "I am strong" or "I am brave" or "I am beautiful" or "I am capable" or anything that is heart-centered and loving toward yourself. Think about your mantra, and let your heart tell you what is right for you. That means that you take the first phrase that comes into your mind that is POSITIVE and write it down—without questioning it, judging it, picking it apart, or sharing it with others. (It is okay to keep your *mantras* private.)

So, let's practice this now. If you feel comfortable closing your eyes, please do so (after you finish reading this paragraph, of course, ☺) and see what mantra comes to mind. It may feel silly at first. And the first thought that comes to mind may even be a negative one. All of that is okay. Whatever comes to mind, be patient and don't judge it. Think about what it is you want to make happen in your life right now—and how you would like to be and feel. You are *not* asking for an object or for stuff. You are *not* asking to become rich and famous. You *are* asking for a feeling or energy to be a part of you in your life right now that would be beneficial to you, that would help you to feel positive about yourself in this moment. Even if you don't believe the thought initially, just say it quietly to yourself several times and see what happens.

Write it down:

I AM _____

If you would like to do so, you can write this mantra and other loving messages to yourself on sticky notes and place them somewhere visible, like on your bathroom mirror or in your journal. The idea is to surround yourself with loving words about YOU.

As you become more tuned in to your thoughts and notice how easy it is to get caught up in negative, judgmental self-talk, you can start to catch yourself and stop by pushing PAUSE IN YOUR BRAIN when the thought arises. Your first daily practice then is to notice your negative thought and replace it with the opposite, positive thought. You can replace it with your mantra.

For example, if you catch yourself thinking that you can't wear those jeans because you would look ugly in them, instead of going down a rabbit hole of negative self-talk, you can push PAUSE IN YOUR BRAIN to stop that particular thought and begin to say to yourself, "I am so much more than the way I look," over and over again. Your mantra can change daily or you can use the same one for a while—whatever will be most helpful to you to begin to be more loving and kind to yourself.

Engaging in loving self-talk is a commitment. Unfortunately, it is generally not encouraged or taught. On a daily basis, and even multiple times a day, we are challenged to find ways to feel good about ourselves because we are bombarded by images of what it means to be "perfect," in terms of physical beauty, talent, intelligence, achievements, and more. It takes strength and courage to stand up to the messaging we receive through these images and words that surround us. Be strong! Be courageous! And stay committed!

Committing to loving self-talk is *not* selfish or egotistical. It does *not* mean you are full of yourself. It is actually the opposite. It *is rooted in love, kindness, and connectedness.* It is *not* about being better than anyone else or trying to get more than others. It is about growing into being more comfortable with who you are, which gives permission to those around you to do the same. In other words, if you begin to feel more comfortable with yourself, that energy will pour out of you and others will begin to feel the same way too.

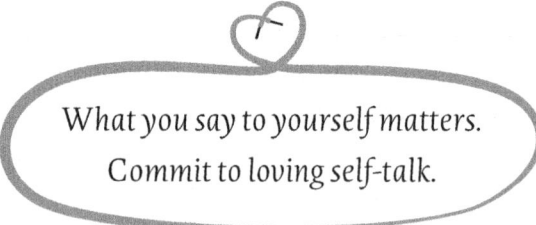

What you say to yourself matters.
Commit to loving self-talk.

2

YOU BELONG BECAUSE
YOU WERE BORN CURIOUS

WHAT DOES IT MEAN TO BE CURIOUS AND THINK CRITICALLY?

We just discussed that it is important to have opinions and think critically. We want to notice our thoughts, to be thoughtful and curious. This is especially important in school.

Being a good student at school is *not* what matters. What matters most is *how* you learn. What matters most is that you *want* to learn. True learning is rooted in curiosity. True learning is being curious about the world, about how things work, about how others live, and about how we treat each other. Thinking critically means you are seeking answers and are open to infinite possibilities. It is a connected curiosity, which is founded in gratitude for your ability to learn and gratitude for those who teach you.

A central pillar of critical thinking is to not take information at face value (believing what you are told without question). This is especially important when you are being told stories by or about others. When you hear a story about someone or when you read something about someone in a text, for example, take a moment to sit with that information. Do not just assume it is true because someone is telling you it is true or because you are reading it in a text or on the internet. This does not mean you should doubt everything everyone says to you; it means that you take the time to think about what is said to you and come to a conclusion for yourself.

"I have no special talent. I am only passionately curious."
~ Albert Einstein

These are perfect moments to practice pushing PAUSE IN YOUR BRAIN to notice where your thoughts are going before you judge another person or before you spread a story around to others. We need time and space to process information. Creating a pause button in your brain that you can work with internally gives you that time and space. It's helpful to visualize your pause button, to actually see it. So, let's do it now, visualizing and giving your pause button a shape, a size, a color.

What shape is the pause button in your brain?_____

What color is it? _____

Does it glow or sparkle? _____

Is there anything else unique about your pause button? If so, describe it. _____

_____

Now that you have created your pause button, it's time to practice using it. Give yourself a moment to stop, to push your pause button; then take a breath and process what you are being told. Pushing pause is especially important when we are involved in drama or gossip. It takes self-discipline and courage not to immediately join in. Be strong and courageous!

The rumor mill is vicious, and it can be detrimental to those involved. Have kindness and compassion for those involved in the story being told. Take a moment to decide what your response is going to be to the story being shared with you—especially when the story you are sharing has nothing to do with you.

If you want to share information or a story about someone else, push your pause button and consider if you could say those EXACT words directly to that person's face (the person whom the story or rumor is about). If you feel like there is NO WAY you could walk up to that person and say everything word-for-word, directly to their face (and then feel good about yourself for saying those words), that is a clear sign to yourself to not spread the story. Do not type the story on your phone or computer. Do not post those words for others to read. Do not tell others the story. Do not hide behind your phone or computer. Hold yourself accountable for what you type, write, and say.

We must all hold ourselves to higher standards, especially when we talk about others. Again, be strong and courageous! Many adults struggle to hold themselves accountable for what they say, write, type, and post. You can help establish better standards for your generation by holding yourself accountable.

With regard to social media, it is important to think about what you post and why, no matter what the topic may be. Before posting anything, consider what kind of attention you are hoping to attract. Is it genuine, real, and positive? Is it how you wish people would perceive you? Does it represent the real you?

It is also important to consider the choices you make about what you watch and listen to on your TV, computer, and phone. Words and images have energy attached to them. We need to be aware of the energy we invite into our hearts and minds. Use your critical thinking skills to decide what you want to invite in. Is it positive, loving energy or negative, violent energy? You deserve to be surrounded by positive, loving energy every day.

Think critically.

3

YOU BELONG BECAUSE
COMPASSION CONNECTS US

WHAT DOES IT MEAN TO HAVE COMPASSION?

When a person shows compassion, they are acknowledging that we are all the same. In knowing that you are not better or worse than anyone else, you can't help but feel sadness for their suffering and joy for their triumphs. This is compassion—the feeling for another's pain or difficulty that opens your heart and enables you to be merciful toward them.

Be merciful toward others and yourself and honor how complicated it is to be human. Having mercy is *not* the same thing as pity. When we feel pity or feel sorry for others, we undermine their experience. And ultimately, we may end up belittling others or thinking less of them. Just as with others, when we feel sorry for ourselves, we undermine our own experience, which can make us think less of ourselves.

We are not just one thing; we are many things. We don't have to just be strong; we can also be soft. I have heard wise people speak of this idea by explaining that we exist in contradiction, that we do not have to live in a "this or that" type of world. We can live in a "this AND that" type of world.

So, what if we can be genuinely kind, compassionate, AND fiercely strong and unwavering—all at the same time? I be-

"Our human compassion binds us the one to the other— not in pity or patronizingly, but as human beings who have learnt how to turn our common suffering into hope for the future."
~ *Nelson Mandela*

lieve we can be kind and have mercy for someone without allowing them to take advantage of us. I believe we can live with a wide-open heart that loves and feels for others and the world AND we can have a strong backbone that allows us to stand up for ourselves. I believe we need to foster a world where we all strive to be compassionate, to be kind. We must start with being kind to ourselves.

Let's go back to the section on loving self-talk, where we talked about *mantras*, the "I am statements," and bring this loving thought into the body. It is important to connect our thoughts to our bodies, which helps us feel compassion for ourselves and others. One way to connect our mind to our body is by making physical contact with our body WHILE thinking. This can be done using a gentle tapping motion. [1]

I invite you to do this now. Using two or three of your fingers, gently begin to tap the center of your forehead,

---

1 This is a variation of Emotional Freedom Technique (EFT)

directly above your eyebrows. While you GENTLY tap the center of your forehead, begin to say your mantra. Repeat your mantra three times.

You can use this technique at any time. It can be done covertly, meaning no one has to notice. For example, if you tap the outside of your hand, as opposed to your forehead, you can do it while you are sitting at your desk, with your hands on your lap. You can say your mantra three times in your head and be done. The point is to connect the mind and body through tapping, while stating a powerful mantra to replace the negativity swirling in your head. This tapping technique can become a daily practice, a daily habit.

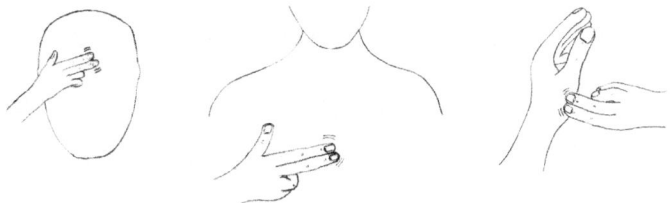

Illustrations by Tristan Kono, age twelve

Three powerful places to tap loving thoughts into your body are at the center of your forehead (your third eye center), the center of your chest (next to your heart), and on the outside of your hand at the base of your thumb. Remember it is a very GENTLE tap.

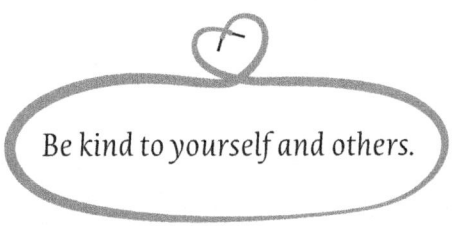

Be kind to yourself and others.

4

YOU BELONG BECAUSE
YOU MAKE MISTAKES.
WE ALL MAKE MISTAKES

WHAT DOES IT MEAN TO BE YOUR BEST SELF?

Being your best self means being the best version of you. It does not mean trying to be like someone else, trying to impress someone else, or trying to please someone else. It means BEING THE REAL YOU. Figuring out the real you takes courage, patience, kindness, and support. Finding the real you is a process—a journey of self-discovery—and it starts from a place of complete and total compassion for yourself.

It is important to be honest as you begin this path toward self-discovery. The ability to do the right thing when no one is looking takes great courage and confidence. It comes from having that strong sense of self, from believing in your SELF. It is important to allow space for self-exploration to help discover that sense of self. Part of the self-discovery journey involves making mistakes. Being honest and being the best version of you is not the same thing as being perfect.

Let yourself be human; let yourself make mistakes. Let yourself fail miserably and find the strength to recover. What if that exact failure was the only way to open a door to a new and amazing chapter in your life?

Redefine what "success" is. Success is generally defined as achieving as much as possible—achieving high academic degrees, achieving high-paying jobs, accumulating money and things, and achieving status (similar to being the most popular). This definition of success is generally what people post on social media. Unfortunately, social media has become a place where people feel the need to portray this image of perfection and highlight their "successes." Yet, the actual reality may be far from that. What if we started posting a more authentic version of our life on social media—one that is in line with a new definition of success?

> "Success is liking yourself, liking what you do, and liking how you do it."
> ~ Maya Angelou

What if being successful has nothing to do with academic or monetary achievement? What if being successful has to do with being YOUR BEST SELF as often as possible? What if being successful is about creating space every day to breathe into your heart so that you feel the love for yourself that then becomes love for others? What if the more we live in our hearts, the more successful we are? And what if that sense of stepping into our heart space is what actually leads us to stepping into life in a way that allows us to find the abundance of support we want? What if we then find the path that is just ours and that path leads us to connect with the friends we want, the support we deserve, and the courage to be our authentic selves every day?

The hardest part of allowing room for us to make mistakes, to be a messy human, is to then forgive ourselves for not being perfect. I believe we are born perfect, but that is not the same thing as having to be perfect. We are born perfect because we come into this life connected to all that is. Part of this intricate connection is our shared experience of messing up, of failing, of not getting things right the first time (or even the first few times), of hurting others and ourselves. Taking responsibility for our words and actions is critical. It is also difficult and takes a great deal of honesty, discipline, and self-compassion.

One way to invite in this practice of self-forgiveness is with a powerful prayer called Ho'oponopono, which is an ancient Hawaiian practice of forgiveness and reconciliation. One of my dear friends introduced me to this practice. It is an incredibly healing way to move through our personal pain and the pain we inevitably cause others.

The practice involves four statements, and it is something you can say over and over to yourself while thinking of the person you are apologizing to, whether it is to yourself or someone else.

I am sorry.
Please forgive me.
Thank you.
I love you.

If this speaks to you, take a moment now to put your hands over your heart, close your eyes, and say these four statements to yourself three times, as you visualize the person to whom you are apologizing. That person may be you. Then take a deep breath and notice what thoughts and feelings come up for you.

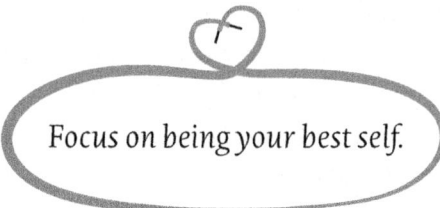

Focus on being your best self.

5

YOU BELONG BECAUSE
YOU ARE POWERFUL

WHAT DOES IT MEAN TO STAY IN YOUR POWER?

You have a bright light shining inside you. This light is your soul, your essence. It is what you came into the world with that makes you YOU. Shine your light on others!

As you practice loving self-talk throughout your day, you will begin to find the inner strength to radiate your light. People will begin to notice your bright, shining light, as it comes from a place of feeling more comfortable in your own skin. It is important to protect that light and stay confident in your power. Your light is your power, and in order to stay in your power, you need to both shine and protect that light.

It is easy to give away your power to others, to give your voice to others, to doubt what you think and feel, and to doubt yourself. Some people may try to dim your light because they are scared by it or disconnected from themselves and from the divine light that shines in all of us. Dimming your light is the same as giving away or letting others take away your power.

Part of staying in your power and not giving it away is to know when someone is trying to get you to disconnect from your light, from your in-

> "The most common way people give up their power is by thinking they don't have any."
> ~ Alice Walker

ner truth, from your heart. Do not let them. It is possible to shine your light, to own yourself completely, to be powerful and not cause harm to others. It is possible to create boundaries that protect you but do not disconnect you from others. Create compassionate, strong boundaries. Do not let people walk all over you or take advantage of you. If you feel exhausted or depleted after spending time with someone, it may be a sign that you are giving away your power, by allowing them to diminish your light.

If the ways in which you are showing up in your life are grounded, or held in the greatest and highest good of yourself and others, you will stay true to what makes you powerful and you will honor the ways in which others are powerful. Knowing how to shine your light and how to protect yourself with compassionate boundaries is an ongoing life practice. We will talk more about how to trust your gut and hone your intuition and your wisdom in the next chapter. This is the life practice that allows us to stay in our power.

As you think about your inner light and your personal power, please remember:

It is okay to say NO.
It is okay to disagree.

It is okay to be the one to stand up for what is right and what is true, even if no one else does. This is how change happens in the world. This is how you empower yourself and others to be heard.

YOU are powerful.
You ARE powerful.
You are POWERFUL.

Now I invite you to say these lines out loud and FEEL the energy of the words. You can place your hands on your belly while you speak:

It is okay to say NO.
It is okay to disagree.

It is okay to be the one to stand up for what
is right and what is true, even if no one else does.
This is how change happens in the world.
This is how I empower MYself and others to be heard.

I am powerful.
I AM powerful.
I am POWERFUL.

Stay in your power.

6

YOU BELONG BECAUSE
WHAT IS BEST FOR YOU
LIES WITHIN YOU

WHAT DOES IT MEAN TO TRUST YOUR GUT?

Our body tells us when something is off—when something is not quite right. We usually feel a strong sensation in our stomach, in our gut. We may feel queasy or nauseous, like our stomach is tied in knots. When we feel excited or nervous about something, we can sometimes experience a fluttering sensation in our belly that is often described as having butterflies in our stomach.

Feeling sensations in our belly is one way our body communicates with us. And when our body communicates with us, we need to listen to it. We just talked about the importance of staying in our power, and various healing traditions teach that our power center is in our gut, in our stomach. Trust your gut! It is your power center.

Part of your daily practice can be to hone your intuition. What is intuition? It is your inner voice, your inner knowing. It can speak to you through your body, especially through your gut. It is important to strengthen your inner voice. Give your intuition time. When your inner voice is speaking to you and trying to get your attention, especially through physical sensations, stop and listen to it.

> "I only do what my gut tells me to. I think it's smart to listen to other people's advice, but at the end of the day, you're the only one who can tell you what's right for you."
> ~ Jennifer Lopez

Sometimes we have two opposing voices in our head. This is depicted in cartoons as an angel on one shoulder and a devil on the other. How do we know which voice to listen to? Our inner light always wants what is best for us. Yet, this angel voice is often the more challenging one to pay attention to. This voice is the one that is asking you to love and protect yourself, the one that is asking you to be kind and connected. It is easy to deny it or push it away so that you do not stand out in a situation, so that you do not make others uncomfortable in a situation. It takes great courage to trust your inner knowing. Be courageous!

We are all born with this wisdom; we just forget. We are also taught to not listen to it, to go with what everyone else says, to conform, to fit in. But in honoring our inner wisdom, we are actually listening to what is in our greatest and highest good. When we do that, we are honoring what is in everyone's greatest and highest good since we are intuitively connected to one another. Connecting and belonging are not the same as fitting in. We will talk about this idea more in Chapter 12.

One way to practice listening to your intuition is to check in with your belly, with your gut, every day. Listen to it. When it tells you something is off, trust it.

One area where your intuition can inform you is regarding relationships and whom you choose to be in relationships with. Be courageously connected to whom you spend time with and what relationships you invest in. If something feels off in a relationship, take time to investigate what is at the root of (underneath) that unease. If your body tells you it is not a healthy or safe relationship, LISTEN to that, honor that, and honor yourself.

Let's talk more about connecting with your body.

Trust your gut.

7

YOU BELONG BECAUSE
YOUR BODY IS SACRED AND BELONGS TO YOU

WHAT IS SACRED?

Sacred means special. It is something that is revered, something that deserves to be honored. Your body is sacred! Listen to your body, believe in your body, and nurture your body.

One of the easiest ways to connect with your body is to connect with what you put into it and how you feel afterward. So, pay attention to the food you eat and what you drink and how it makes you feel.

Each time you put food and drink into your body, feel into how your body receives it. For instance, the next time you drink a glass of water, notice how your body feels immediately after you drink it. Then, the next time you drink a glass of soda or juice, do the same thing and notice how your body feels afterward. Remember that you are notic-ing sensation, *not taste*. How does your belly FEEL a few minutes after each drink? Overall, does your body feel bet-ter or worse than before you drank it?

You can practice this exercise with healthy food ver-sus unhealthy food too. Your body will let you know which foods make you feel stron-ger and more vitalized and which foods make you feel sluggish and lethargic, may-be even leaving you with a stomachache or a bloated feeling. We are often drawn to "unhealthy" foods be-cause they smell and taste so good. But if those foods make us feel bad afterward, it's our body's way of letting us know they really aren't good for us.

> "No one's body is up for comment. No matter how small, how curvy, how round, how flat. If you love you, then I love you."
> ~ *Shonda Rhimes*

This daily practice is a body-centered practice. It in-volves being in your body. The more you pay attention to your body, such as noticing how your body feels after you drink water versus soda, the more you are IN YOUR BODY. And the more you are IN YOUR BODY, the less you will be in your head, in your thoughts.

So, let's try a body-centered practice now . . .

Just for a moment, put one hand on your heart and one hand on your belly. Close your eyes or lower your gaze and take three deep breaths. Feel the air fill up your lungs and belly as you inhale, and feel the softening that hap-pens as you exhale and release. If finding a deep breath is hard, that is okay. If you are physically uncomfortable, that is okay too. A huge part of finding a daily practice is being okay with where you are.

Sometimes we feel calm and rooted, like we are standing on solid, safe ground. In those moments, being in our body and connected to our breath feels good. At other times, we are exhausted, scared, sad, anxious, or overwhelmed, and being in our body and connected to our breath is difficult. If that is where you are right now, allow that to be okay. Invite that energy to move through and out by wiggling your body, by moving your head, your shoulders, your hips, and your hands and feet as little or as much as you want. Gently or vigorously shake it out and then breathe again. As you release this energy, give yourself permission to feel what you feel without judging it, or trying to make sense of it, or even trying to make it go away.

It is imperative to move your body every day. There are so many different ways to move: walking, running, playing sports, dancing, biking, skating, hiking, yoga, lifting your arms to stretch while you are seated, etc. Welcome movement, especially when you feel like your thoughts are racing or when you are having intense, uncomfortable emotions that feel as though they are stuck in your body.

By committing to a daily, body-centered practice that involves movement and breath, you are also telling yourself that YOU MATTER and that YOUR BODY BELONGS TO YOU. It does not belong to anyone else. It is not for others to do with what they want. It is not for others to judge or criticize. It is not for others to hurt or abuse in any way. The ways in which you physically touch yourself, and the ways in which others physically touch you, must be rooted in kindness, compassion, and connection.

A daily body scan can also help you feel more IN your body and can help you notice where you hold tension or feel tight and where you feel open and more flexible. We store emotions, memories, and energy in our bodies. Our bodies tell us how we are doing. Our bodies do not lie. They reveal what is true. We just need to allow the time and space to be connected, so we can listen.

A daily body scan requires very little time. You can start with a one-minute practice every morning. Here are the basic steps:

- When you wake up, place your feet OR your sits bones on the Earth (on the floor of your bedroom).

- Feel the connection to what is beneath you. Notice the temperature.

- Now feel the connection to your body. Start with your toes. Feel each toe.

- Then move up through your toes, feeling and noticing each part of your body.

- Move up through the top of your head.

- As you connect with different body parts, move them and take note of how they feel. If they are tired or hurt, send them breath.

- Take three deep breaths, feeling each breath as it moves from your toes all the way up through the crown of your head.

- Say "thank you" to your body each time you breathe in.

- Step into your day connected to your body, your breath, and the Earth. This daily practice can remind you that your body is sacred and it belongs to you.

Remember:

YOUR body is sacred
Your BODY is sacred
Your body is SACRED

Your body matters
YOU matter
Your body houses your light, your soul, your essence.
Honor that container

Move your body daily:
Stretch
Lift your head up
Lift your chest up
Wiggle
Dance
Dance
Dance

Honor your body.

8

YOU BELONG BECAUSE
YOU NEED QUIET MOMENTS
WE ALL NEED QUIET MOMENTS

HOW DO WE CREATE SACRED SPACE IN OUR LIVES?

We have discussed several tools you can use every day to connect with yourself. Let's talk about how to create a sacred space, a place where you feel comfortable working with these tools. Creating a special physical space in your home, or your room, is a way to be with yourself and take time out of your day to focus on you, to listen to your heart, and to notice what is happening in your life.

Do you have a special place in your home, in your room, or somewhere outside—a special place where you can have quiet reflection time WITHOUT technology being around? This may be difficult to find because of where you live or how many people share your home with you, but it is possible. It can even be a public place, like a library or a park. The invitation here is to create your very own sacred space, where you can slow down and be alone with yourself.

The idea is to have a special physical space that allows you to create sacred space in your head—sacred space for quiet and for reflection and for breathing into your heart. By creating sacred space for ourselves, we can more easily create sacred space in our conversations—space to ac-

> "In a gentle way, you can shake the world."
> ~ Mahatma Gandhi

tually listen to what others are saying and sacred pauses before responding to others. By creating sacred space, we allow for true connection with ourselves and to others.

Sacred space means device-free. That being said, music and guided meditation, as well as some really amazing apps, can help us ground and breathe and find that connection. There is a time and place for using our devices to support us in becoming more rooted. However, we really need to practice putting down our phones as much as possible.

One way to take a break from electronics is to put your phone and all other electronic devices "to bed" at night. Allow your mind time to truly rest. Sleep is critical. This takes a ton of willpower and courage because it may upset people who try to get ahold of you at all hours of the day and night. But, by doing this for yourself, you may also give others permission to disconnect from their devices, so they can actually connect to themselves.

Most of us are in great need of sacred space and quiet reflection time. Sometimes we need to create a physical reminder to help us take that sacred time for ourselves. For instance, you may want to create an altar, a special place in a corner of your room or on a shelf or table where you can place important photos, quotes, poems, items such as rocks or stones, or other things that have great meaning for you. This altar can be the place where you allow yourself to sit and be present with what is happening in your life and to step into your daily practices in an uninterrupted way. This special place can serve as a reminder that there is beauty and sacredness all around you.

Take a moment now to write down what you want your sacred space to look like.

You can use these questions as prompts or write whatever comes to you…

Where is it going to be? _____

_____

_____

What material things will be there?_____

_____

_____

_____

Will you create an altar? _____ If so, what will it look like?

_____

_____

_____

_____

How will you keep your space free from distractions, including noise and clutter? _____

_____

_____

What colors and images do you want surrounding you?

_____

_____

_____

What are you going to do in your sacred space? _____

_____

_____

How often will you visit your sacred space? _____

_____

Create sacred space and
SLOW DOWN.

9

YOU BELONG BECAUSE
YOUR BREATH AND INTENTION ARE YOUR MOST POWERFUL TOOLS

WHAT IS INTENTION?

Intention is desire. It is your hope. It is what you hope and want to have happen. It is your will—what you desire to manifest in your life. It is not the same as what you expect to have happen or what you think should happen. It is what you want to attract into your life. It is using your very powerful mind and your very powerful thoughts to create the goodness you want to see in your life. When we combine our intentions with our breath, when we breathe intentionally and purposefully (on purpose and with awareness of what we wish to create in our lives), we use our most powerful tools.

Intention is heart-centered, meaning it is not related to matters of the head but to matters of the heart. It is based in love and compassion, based in the greatest and highest good of yourself and others. Heart-centered intention is powerful. It is the energy you put out into the universe. It is stating loudly and clearly what you want in your life.

We are not asking for all the money in the world or fame or anything that may cause harm to another. We are asking for support to pursue our dreams.

> "Feelings come and go like clouds in a windy sky. Conscious breathing is my anchor."
> ~ Thich Nhat Hanh

We are willing the universe to support us in what it is that we love, in supporting our "soul purpose," our reason for being here. The most powerful way to state your intentions is to do it while asking for ease and grace AND while breathing. This purposeful breath brings us back to our bodies, back to our heart, and back to the bright light shining inside.

So far, we've discussed several powerful tools that you can use, such as a daily body scan. I believe that our two MOST POWERFUL TOOLS are our breath and intention. Can you take these two tools and commit to using them daily? Can you commit to taking sixty seconds every day to come into your body WITH your breath? And what if you don't have sixty seconds? What if you have ten seconds? Can you take ten seconds first thing in the morning to place your feet on the floor, or sit on the floor, and find your breath? To take one hand to your belly and one hand to your heart and breathe love and bright colorful light into your heart? Just one big purposeful breath. And with that big powerful breath, state your intention, either out loud or silently to yourself.

Let's do this now. Take a moment to find your breath. Once you find a slower and deeper breath, set an intention to pause more frequently throughout your day to notice how your body feels. Most of us could benefit from starting with this intention practice. As you slowly breathe in and out, say your intention silently to yourself, "My intention is to pause and notice how my body feels several times throughout my day, with ease and grace." I invite you to do this for the rest of today. Whenever the thought comes to you, whenever you remember your intention to pause and pay attention to how your body feels, do so with one deep breath. See how the day goes with that intention being supported by your breath.

This is a simple, yet powerful, intention. It is an intention for one day that may stretch out over several days. Your intentions can grow from there to include other intentions, such as to feel more at peace throughout the day with ease and grace, to have the courage to shine your light more throughout the day with ease and grace, to hear your intuition clearly throughout the day with ease and grace, to steer clear of drama and negative energy throughout your day with ease and grace, to reach out for more support at school without fear and judgment throughout the day with ease and grace, etc. Each time you state your intention, your powerful breath is its companion.

Pausing to breathe can allow space for us to heal. This is why it is one of our most powerful tools. Healing comes from dropping into our body and into our heart space. Healing comes from moments of being present and connected. Our purposeful breath is what brings us to the present and connects us. We are all healing on some level, meaning we are all working through sad, painful, and traumatic experiences at varying levels of intensity at different times in our life.

We can find these healing moments first thing in the morning. We can find these healing moments in the sacred space we create. We can find these healing moments throughout the day, if we commit to a practice of noticing more often—noticing the color of the sky, noticing the feel of the air, noticing how our body feels when we wake up.

My intention to find my body—to feel and notice my body throughout the day with my purposeful breath—was the most powerful practice I discovered after losing my younger brother. So many people helped me during that dark time. Yet, finding my yoga practice, which is a practice of intentionally being in your body with your breath, became my lifeline. It was the way I was able to find small moments of healing, moments of really connecting with my feelings and moving them through my body, instead of being taken over by my feelings.

The only thing that we truly have control over is our breath, and by connecting to our breath, we have control over how we respond to what unfolds in life. For some, the breath might be limited by physical ailments or conditions, such as asthma. Even in that limited space, our heart-focused practice is always available to us. Our intentions and our *mantras* are always available to us. The more we practice using these tools, the more readily available they are to us, and the more easily we can access them in times of anger, sadness, fear, and doubt.

Practice daily.

10

YOU BELONG BECAUSE
YOU ARE ENOUGH

WHAT DOES IT MEAN TO BE ENOUGH?

It means that you are enough exactly the way you are. It means that you are beautiful exactly the way you are. It means that you were born whole and perfect, no matter how the moment of your birth unfolded. It means you are still whole, even if you feel broken. It means you are still perfect, even if sad things have happened. You are enough, beautiful, whole, and perfect because you are the ONLY YOU, because you are connected to the rest of the world, because YOU ARE MEANT TO BE.

We MUST stop comparing ourselves to others. This is NEVER helpful. Looking up to someone, admiring someone, being inspired by someone—these are all amazing ways to feel. They help us push ourselves and strive for more. But that is not the same thing as wanting to BE someone else or thinking that we have to be like someone

else or that we have to look like someone else to be worth-
while. Body comparisons are especially toxic. Yet, in our
society, this is very difficult to avoid. In daily life, most people seem to be hyper-focused on these ideas of beauty and
what it means to be de-
sirable. These are just
ideas—not the way we
need to be. It is up to us
to decide to not sub-
scribe to these ideas, to
not agree with them.

> "You can be whatever size you are,
> and you can be beautiful both
> inside and out. We're always told
> what's beautiful and what's not,
> and that's not right."
> ~ Serena Williams

It is common to feel
self-conscious about your physical appearance and about
how others perceive you. It can be difficult to believe in
yourself, so the invitation here is to bring in the thought
that you are enough in this exact moment in time. What
matters MOST is your opinion of yourself.

Obviously, this is so much easier said than done. Once
again, it takes daily practice to not get sucked into this
toxic idea of striving for physical beauty above all else.
The daily practice of connecting to what is real, to what
is important, is found through your heart, through your
breath, through breathing into your body and feeling
your connection to all that is. When you are in that connected space, you can feel that you are enough exactly as
you are in this moment and realize that the most common definition of what it means to be beautiful and successful is rooted in the mind, in limited thinking, in fear
of being left out, left alone, or judged by others. This is all
fear-based, and it is not what matters. Living in your heart
and connecting to your mind through your heart is how

to remember that you are enough. You have a reason for being, and that reason is rooted in love.

HOW do we practice feeling like we are enough?

One way to do this is through connected breath. We have talked about our breath being one of our most powerful tools. We went through a very similar breath practice already. Let's do another one that is focused on being enough, on building confidence in who we are.

Place one hand on your heart and one hand on your belly, or both hands on your heart. Your hands don't have to be in one specific place. What's most important is that you are connecting the palms of your hands to your body. Once you have your hands on your heart or on your heart and belly, close your eyes or lower your eye gaze. Start to notice where your breath is. See if you can slow and deepen your breath. Or start to invite your breath to move more slowly and deeply.

To begin, breathe in through your nose and out your mouth. Then see if you can breathe in and out through your nose. The intent is to feel your chest and belly RISE on your INHALE. In other words, you want your belly and chest to push against your hands as you breathe in. Then, feel your chest and belly SOFTEN as you EXHALE. In other words, feel your belly and chest go down as you breathe out.

It may take several moments to find this deep, connected breath. There is no rush. It is okay if it doesn't happen the first time or the first several times. Stick with it and see if you can eventually count your breath in and count your breath out. Counting will give your mind something to focus on.

A slow count to four is a good place to start. Inhale to the count of four and exhale to the count of four. Do three rounds of this. Now inhale to the count of four, hold your breath for two counts at the top of your inhale, and exhale to the count of six. When your mind goes somewhere else, bring it back to counting. Now breathe in the words, "I am enough," three times.

Your breath is powerful, and your thoughts are powerful. Once again, bring those two powers together.

You are enough. Believe it.

11

YOU BELONG BECAUSE
YOU ARE NEVER ALONE

HOW DO YOU KNOW YOU ARE NEVER ALONE?

It is completely normal to have times when you feel alone. Most of us experience feeling lonely—feeling like no one understands us, like no one cares, like we don't belong. We ALL feel these feelings in different ways at different times. What we must work to remember is that we are *not* ever alone. We are always connected to something greater, and because of that, we are always being held.

In those moments when you feel alone, lost, or misunderstood, the practice is to find your breath, find your center, find your heart, and connect to the energy that flows through every living being. Various cultural traditions and practices, such as yoga, talk about the idea of a shared life force, sometimes called *prana* or *qi* (Pronounced "Chee"). Every living being has this life force, this energy, running through it that goes beyond the physical body. This energy is something that we intuitively feel about one another. It gets our attention through sensations in the body, such as shivers down the spine (when it is an uncomfortable energy) or butterflies in the stomach (when it is an affectionate energy).

This energy remains even after someone dies. I feel my brother's loving energy around me quite often. I call upon his life force to protect and guide me.

> "I was born by myself but carry the spirit and blood of my father, mother, and my ancestors. So I am really never alone. My identity is through that line."
> ~ Ziggy Marley

The more you practice connecting to your heart and breath on a daily basis, the more easily you can access this connected energy in times of loneliness and confusion. The more you feel into the possibility that we are all connected, the more you can call upon that energy to support you. This may sound strange because it is not something you can see or touch. But you can learn to feel it.

When you step into this practice of connecting to your heart and breath every day, you start to notice the energy you send out and the energy others are sending toward you. You may also notice the energy coming from the plants and trees and from animals. If you have a pet, they definitely give off energy. It may be calming, soothing, and loving energy, or it may be anxious and unsettling. The more you work with this concept (that energy is a part of everything), the more the ideas that we are never alone and that we are always connected by this invisible energy will begin to resonate with you, empower you, and support you.

There are generations and generations of people who were here before us. Family members and community members, very powerful healers and prophets, people you may know about from studying history, or family and friends you knew in this lifetime who have died. All of these people are your ancestors, and they are available to guide you and protect you ALL of the time. You just need to ask for their guidance and support.

You can do that through prayer or through stating an intention. Prayer is just a sacred way of talking to someone, to a greater power, to family and friends no longer physically here. Prayer is stating intention in a sacred and connected way. You can say your prayer or write it in the form of a letter or poem or journal entry. It can be as simple as, "Dear ancestors, please guide me in a loving and safe way," or "Dear ancestors, please surround me with love and light and help me to remember I am not alone."

Just as we are connected to universal energy, we can put intentions and questions out to the universe, out to our ancestors. Be bold and clear with your words and trust that IF it is in your greatest and highest good, THEN it will be in the greatest and highest good of all.

We do not call upon our ancestors for specific things. We do not ask them to save us from suffering and pain. Nor do we ask for material items to be given to us. We are asking for support, for guidance, for love and connection. We are asking for help in listening to what is within our own hearts. We are asking to know when we need to reach out and ask for help from others in the form of friendship, counsel, or professional mental health support.

Asking for guidance can also help us better tune into our intuition and inner guidance because our inner voice is connected to the collective conscious, to the knowledge that is within all of us, even if we don't believe it or understand it.

There is one other very important concept to remember: your ancestors do not need to be blood-related to connect to you or to be a strong presence in your life. Sometimes it is painful to connect to blood relatives, whether living or deceased, because of abuse and other horrible experiences that have taken place. And sometimes, because of life experiences, we are no longer with our blood families. For example, my daughters are both adopted. I believe they are connected to their blood family, as well as to me and to their lifetime forever family, through spirit, not just genetics. Our ancestors are exactly that, OURS. Genetics and blood are not what connect us on a soul level. Love and light are what connect us.

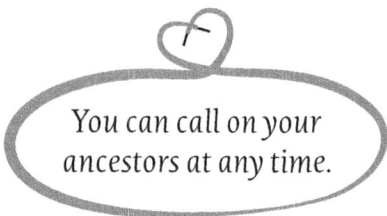

You can call on your
ancestors at any time.

12

YOU BELONG BECAUSE
YOU ARE THE ONLY YOU

WE ASK AGAIN, "WHAT DOES IT MEAN TO BELONG?"

I have often struggled to feel like I belong, like I am "normal," like I fit in. I have listened to wise people, including Brené Brown, talk about this idea: that fitting in is not the same as belonging. Most of us have a strong desire to fit in, to be accepted by others. This desire is rooted in our biological need to be accepted by others so that we can physically survive. In other words, our ancestors, or those who came before us, had to fit in so that other people would take care of them. We, as humans, depended on each other to survive. We still do. But the idea of belonging is different.

Belonging is not the same as being accepted by others. It is about how we feel in our OWN bodies. It is about how we belong to this greater energy that connects us all. It is not about belonging to a certain group or a certain tribe or a certain religion or a certain set of beliefs. It is about belonging to life itself. It is about how we belong to our life, to our life's journey. It is about discovering what it means to be human, and it starts by coming home to ourselves.

What does that mean exactly?

It means moving out of our head—our thoughts, our emotions—and into our heart. This happens through mind, body, and spirit connection, which happens through our intentional breath.

HOW do we do that?

There are several ways to do it, but the most important way is

> "Courage starts with showing up and letting ourselves be seen."
> ~ Brené Brown

one that we have already discussed throughout the book: creating a daily habit of connection, of noticing, of sensing, of being in the present moment. Some call this type of practice "mindfulness." Some call this "contemplative practice." "Mindfulness" is a word that is fairly prevalent right now. When we talk about creating a daily habit of connection, we are essentially talking about creating a mindfulness practice. My two favorite definitions of mindfulness are the following:

- "Paying attention in a particular way: on purpose, in the moment."—Jon Kabat-Zinn
- "Actively noticing new things."—Ellen Langer

Whether you call your practice mindfulness or contemplative or something else, the title is not important; the commitment to what works for you is the key. We have already mentioned some tools you can use, such as tapping in a mantra with an intentional breath. The key is to keep practicing these mindfulness tools, to keep using them.

At this point, I want to say that finding this connection, dropping into our bodies, and moving from our mind into our body and heart is REALLY, REALLY hard. It may sound simple, but simple does not mean easy. And, in general, it is not what we are encouraged to do. This is the work of a lifetime. And, even though it is very difficult, it is POWERFUL and AMAZING and WORTH IT. If we commit to this practice of coming home to ourselves, we give ourselves the gift of living a more connected, more authentic life.

One of the most courageous things we can do is accept ourselves fully, the light and the dark, our bright side and our shadow side, especially when other people are not open to and accepting of us. This is much easier said than done. There is constant pressure to fit in, to not be too different, to not stand out, to conform to standards of beauty and success. It takes incredible courage to not give in to that pressure, to not get caught up in what everyone else thinks, in what everyone else is saying, in what everyone else is doing.

The thing that everyone else might not realize is that an amazing transformation occurs when we decide to fully accept ourselves—when we accept both our inner light and the shadow parts of ourselves, those parts that most everyone tries to keep hidden. When we decide to belong to ourselves first, to fully accept the ALL of who we are, we get to live this "one wild and precious life" more fully, with more authenticity, more realness, and with a deeper sense of freedom. And we don't do it alone. This transformation helps us to wake up to the knowledge that we are connected to everyone, that we need each other to navigate being human together. We realize that we belong to each other, that we belong to the Earth, that we belong to every living being.

Belonging to each other has nothing to do with ownership, in terms of possessions. It means we are truly connected in complete and total equality. No one person is better than another. No one person deserves more than another. We all deserve to feel love and to be cared for. Every living being, including the Earth, deserves to be loved and cared for.

This idea of belonging is big. It goes against what we are taught by dominant society. It goes against judgmental, divisive thinking. We are raised to compete with one another, to be better than one another, to compare ourselves to one another, and to figure out how we can be successful in life, successful meaning financially wealthy and praised by others. And even though we are taught to be better than others, we are also taught that we must fit in, that we must conform to what is expected of us, that we must not shine too brightly or stand out too much. Not only is this confusing, unhealthy, and limiting, it is what disconnects us from our hearts and from each other.

Finally, a big piece of this journey toward belonging to ourselves is having faith that who we are will be revealed to us over time. We need time alone, time to reflect, time to have quiet. We need to SLOW DOWN and create sacred space to be. This is how we come to know more about who we are. Trusting in why we are here, even if we don't know why, is found through slowing down and our daily breathing practice. And if our struggle to feel into who we are becomes overwhelming, we look to others for support and guidance. We are not meant to walk this path alone. IT IS ALWAYS OKAY TO REACH OUT FOR HELP AND SUPPORT!

HOW do we practice belonging to ourselves first?

Take a few moments now to write down or draw out what that means to you. Here are some questions that might help with this writing/drawing exercise:

What does belonging mean to you?

Have there been times in your life when you felt like you belonged? _____

If yes, where did you sense those feelings in your body? For example, "When I have felt like I belonged, my breath moved freely in and out of my body and my feet felt more connected to the ground."

Have there been times in your life when you felt like you did not belong? _____

If yes, where did you sense those feelings in your body? For example, "When I have felt like I did NOT belong, my shoulders and jaw got tight, I began to sweat, my face sometimes turned red with embarrassment, and my stomach was in knots."

Belong to yourself first.

13

YOU BELONG BECAUSE
YOU ARE DIVINE!

WHAT DOES IT MEAN TO BE DIVINE?

When I asked Siri what it means to be divine, I was led to vocabulary.com, which states "divine basically means relating to, coming from, or like God or a god." The word "god" may resonate with you, may speak to you, or may turn you off completely. The idea of God is not necessarily about religion. The idea of God, or a higher power, is about how we all came to be, how we attempt to understand life and death. This idea of a higher power, or believing that there is something greater than us, whether you name it God or Source or Great Spirit, is the very thing that leads to the understanding that there is something connecting us all. We are inextricably linked to each other and to this greater power, this divine light, and it is my belief that this connection is what we are here to remember.

The more we can see and feel that connection, the more settled we feel in our own skin. The more we feel that we are here for a reason, even if we have no idea what that reason is, the more we trust in the divine plan for our life.

> "Beauty is a light in the heart."
> ~ Kahlil Gibran

How exactly do we find that belief—that knowing, that faith—when horrible things happen? We must meet ourselves with compassion and grace, with gentleness and kindness, and allow ourselves time to be with all that we feel. We must surrender to what we are feeling.

Surrender is not the same as giving UP; it is giving IN. We give IN to what we are feeling, so we can process, soften, and ultimately integrate all that we experience. Surrender to who you are meant to be, soften into your true essence, your radiance, your bright light, your heart.

This is another way of saying "let go"; trust in what is and what is to come. This is not giving up; it is a giving over—a giving over to the unknown, to the great mystery of life. This great mystery of life is where the proverbial "Why me?" question is never answered. Life is full of sadness and pain. Avoiding sadness and pain is tempting. Getting stuck in wondering, "Why me?" is a way of avoiding the pain.

Often the reason we are so judgmental and mean to others is because we do not want to be with our own sadness and pain. The most remarkable gift you can give yourself is an invitation to all that you feel. Invite it in, so it can move through you, so it does not stay stuck in your body.

The invitation to PAUSE and feel what we feel, feel it in our bodies, and notice those sensations is what allows us to integrate so that we do not stay stuck in the darkness. The idea is that we can FEEL OUR FEELINGS without becoming our feelings. This may be confusing, but all this means is if we can BE with our feelings in the moment, give them time to be felt in our bodies, then we can acknowledge them and ask them to move through us, instead of having them keep a hold on us in a way that is disempowering and overwhelming.

We get to be human, to be messy, to make mistakes, AND to recover from them, knowing that we are all working to remember who we truly are. This is not an easy task. This is the work of a lifetime, but the more we invite this in, the more alive we become and the brighter our light shines. And shining YOUR light is what it means to be divine.

Take a few moments to think about and answer the following questions:

What does it mean to shine your light? _____

_____

_____

_____

Now, what does that feel like? _____

_____

_____

_____

Have there been times when you felt divine? _____ When you felt that we are all connected? _____ If you answered "yes" to one or both of these questions, describe how you felt and what else you experienced at those times? _____

_____

_____

If nothing comes to mind right now, that is okay. Come back to these questions as often as you like and see what you discover. The invitation here is to connect—to connect to your light, to your breath, to your heart, and to allow your light to pour out to others, as you stay strong and true to yourself. Remember...YOU ARE DIVINE!

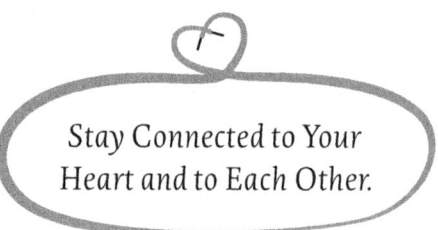

Stay Connected to Your Heart and to Each Other.

CONCLUSION

Now that we have looked at the thirteen reasons why you belong, I encourage you to pick at least one that really speaks to you. Spend some time thinking about why it resonates with you and maybe journal about those thoughts. Of course, you can go back to any and all of the thirteen reasons as often as you wish. They will be here for you always.

I encourage you to stick with these tools and practices too (I've included a toolkit at the end of the book) or find other mindfulness tools to help you commit to a daily practice that is focused on being more loving and kind to yourself and others. This can be your new daily challenge. Challenge yourself to breathe into your heart every day, #lovingbreathchallenge.

I believe a daily practice can help you continue to navigate your adolescence with a knowing that you belong. It is normal to forget this, even to forget multiple times throughout your day. However, contemplative practices can bring you back to remembering your connection.

We are all on this journey together, and when you need extra support, reach out. You do not have to figure it all out on your own. It is okay to make mistakes! It is okay to mess up and to be confused. It is okay to get help, guid-

> "If we have no peace, it is because we have forgotten that we belong to each other."
> ~ Mother Teresa

ance, and counsel. Sometimes the most courageous thing you can do is to ask for help. We find peace, knowing we are in this together. Honor what your heart is asking for.

Breathe into your heart every day, so you feel into your own light. Allow for your light to help others. This is "your one wild and precious life." Claim it!

You are here to shine your light.

You are here on purpose.

Our world needs you!

You are never alone.

Let yourself be bright!

You are divine!

Claim your SELF

Claim your body

Claim your light

Claim your life

Claim THIS life

YOU BELONG!

WHAT ONE THING CAN YOU START TODAY?

Start with this body scan practice:

- When you wake up OR before you go to bed, place your feet OR your sits bones on the Earth (on the floor of your bedroom).

- Feel the connection to what is beneath you. Notice the temperature.

- Now feel the connection to your body. Start with your toes. Feel each toe.

- Then move up through your toes, feeling and noticing each part of your body.

- Move up through the top of your head.

- As you connect with different body parts, move them and take note of how they feel. If they are tired or hurt, send them breath.

- Place your hands on your heart. Take three deep breaths, opening up your lungs and belly, feeling each breath as it moves from your toes all the way up through the crown of your head.

- This is your #lovingbreathchallenge. I challenge you to do this every day for one week and notice how it affects you and those around you.

TOOLKIT

Tools and practices introduced in each chapter:

- Mantra practice—I AM statements (Chapter 1)
- PAUSE BUTTON in your brain (Chapter 2)
- Tapping technique (Chapter 3)
- Ho'oponopono practice (Chapter 4)
- I AM POWERFUL practice (Chapter 5)
- Body-centered breath practice (Chapter 6)
- Body scan (Chapter 7)
- Creating sacred space (Chapter 8)
- Intention practice (Chapter 9)
- I AM ENOUGH breath practice (Chapter 10)
- Connecting with your ancestors through prayer (Chapter 11)
- Writing/drawing exercise about belonging (Chapter 12)
- Writing exercise about being divine (Chapter 13)

OTHER IMPORTANT DAILY PRACTICES

- Move your body every day
- Get more sleep
- Drink more water
- Spend less time on screens
- Eat whole, real food
- Hold your body up and open your heart to the sky

ACKNOWLEDGMENTS

Selecia, Adalea, and Kahlil, you are my teachers, my love, and my light. I love you all more than I ever thought possible. I cannot imagine my life without the three of you bright, beautiful, divine beings. Thank you for allowing me to become a mom, to be YOUR mom.

Bryan, my beloved, you are my everything.

Mom, thank you for teaching me the power of ceremony and ritual.

Dad, thank you for teaching me the power of emotional expression and vulnerability.

Jason, thank you for teaching me the power of being real and living openheartedly.

Matt, thank you for BEING ... your light is forever bright. I know you stay close and help guide us. I miss you and love you forever.

Tammy, thank you for being my spiritual teacher. I am so grateful for you.

Donna and Polly, thank you for your guidance and wisdom.

I have immense gratitude for my community of family and friends ... for ALL THE brilliant and powerful women who walk this path with me, who guide and love me, who radiate love. Thank you especially for your words of wisdom and love for Selecia upon her thirteenth birthday. YOU inspired this book. I love you ALL and am forever grateful for you, my soul sisters!

Thank you to all of my guides and teachers, both here in the physical world and beyond.

ABOUT THE AUTHOR

Tara Emrick grew up in Colorado with her two brothers. She met her husband at Occidental College, where she majored in women's studies. She received her master's degree in social work at San Jose State University and worked with several nonprofits that supported youth.

Tara began teaching yoga for grief after she lost her younger brother in 2006. She is currently working with others to address the impact of trauma and grief on middle school and high school students by implementing healing somatic practices. This new venture is called The HIP ME Project.

Tara lives with her husband and three children in Denver. She speaks to young people, parents, and educators about empowering our teens to embody themselves. If you would like Tara to speak to your group, please contact her at info@hipmepublishing.com.

Made in the USA
Las Vegas, NV
16 February 2021